BEST TEAM EVER 👍

> *"Keep taking chances - make life a beautiful experience and never give up"*

Date: /   /

THINGS TO BE GRATEFUL FOR TODAY

"Have dreams and dream big! Dream without fear"

Date: /   /

THINGS TO BE GRATEFUL FOR TODAY

"Believe in miracles but above all believe in yourself!"

Date: /   /

THINGS TO BE GRATEFUL FOR TODAY

"Let your dreams be as big as your desire to succeed"

Date: /   /

THINGS TO BE GRATEFUL FOR TODAY

> *"Never downgrade your dreams, reach for the stars and believe in your self power"*

Date: /   /

THINGS TO BE GRATEFUL FOR TODAY

> *"They say I dream too big. I say they think too small"* - Unknown

Date: /   /

THINGS TO BE GRATEFUL FOR TODAY

> *"Never be afraid to start something new, if you fail it is just temporary, if you believe and persist you will succeed"*

Date: /   /

THINGS TO BE GRATEFUL FOR TODAY

> *"Your driving force and your power lies within you and the size of your dreams, never give up!"*

Date: /   /

THINGS TO BE GRATEFUL FOR TODAY

> *"Wherever you go, go with all your heart."*
> *- Confucius*

Date: /   /

THINGS TO BE GRATEFUL FOR TODAY

"Together we can achieve more"

Date: /   /

THINGS TO BE GRATEFUL FOR TODAY

> *"Your dreams and your goals are the seeds of your own success"*

Date: /   /

THINGS TO BE GRATEFUL FOR TODAY

"Never give up, keep going no matter what!"

Date: /   /

THINGS TO BE GRATEFUL FOR TODAY

> *"Start where you are and take chances"*

Date: /   /

THINGS TO BE GRATEFUL FOR TODAY

> *"If you never give up you become unbeatable, just keep going!"*

Date: /   /

THINGS TO BE GRATEFUL FOR TODAY

> *"Life isn't about finding yourself. Life is about creating yourself."* - George Bernard Shaw

Date: /   /

THINGS TO BE GRATEFUL FOR TODAY

> *"Change your life today. Don't gamble on the future, act now, without delay."* — Simone de Beauvoir

Date: /   /

THINGS TO BE GRATEFUL FOR TODAY

> *"Keep your motivation and your momentum with a new goal every day!"*

Date: /   /

THINGS TO BE GRATEFUL FOR TODAY

> *"Aim for the stars to keep your dreams alive"*

Date: /   /

THINGS TO BE GRATEFUL FOR TODAY

"When life gives you lemons, add a little gin and tonic"

Date: /   /

THINGS TO BE GRATEFUL FOR TODAY

> *"There are no limits to what you can achieve if you believe in your dreams"*

Date: /   /

THINGS TO BE GRATEFUL FOR TODAY

> *"When you feel you are defeated, just remember, you have the power to move on, it is all in your mind"*

Date: /   /

THINGS TO BE GRATEFUL FOR TODAY

"Don't just dream your dreams, make them happen!"

Date: /   /

THINGS TO BE GRATEFUL FOR TODAY

"Opportunity comes to those who never give up"

Date: /   /

THINGS TO BE GRATEFUL FOR TODAY

"*You are the creator of your own opportunities*"

Date: /   /

THINGS TO BE GRATEFUL FOR TODAY

> *"Always aim for bigger goals, they have the power to keep you motivated"*

Date: /   /

THINGS TO BE GRATEFUL FOR TODAY

> *"Success is not a place or a destination, it is a way of thinking while always having a new goal in mind"*

Date: /   /

THINGS TO BE GRATEFUL FOR TODAY

> *"Every achievement starts with a dream and a goal in mind"*

Date: /   /

THINGS TO BE GRATEFUL FOR TODAY

> *"Change the world one dream at a time, believe in your dreams"*

Date: /   /

THINGS TO BE GRATEFUL FOR TODAY

> *"Never loose confidence in your dreams, there will be obstacles and defeats, but you will always win if you persist"*

Date: /   /

THINGS TO BE GRATEFUL FOR TODAY

> *""Never wait for someone else to validate your existence, you are the creator of your own destiny"*

Date: /   /

THINGS TO BE GRATEFUL FOR TODAY

"Dreams are the energy that power your life"

Date: /   /

THINGS TO BE GRATEFUL FOR TODAY

> *"Dreams make things happen, nothing is impossible as long as you believe."* - Anonymous

Date: /   /

THINGS TO BE GRATEFUL FOR TODAY

"Always dream big and follow your heart"

Date: /   /

THINGS TO BE GRATEFUL FOR TODAY

"Never stop dreaming." - Anonymous

Date: /   /

THINGS TO BE GRATEFUL FOR TODAY

> *"Everything you dream is possible as long as you believe in yourself"*

Date: / /

THINGS TO BE GRATEFUL FOR TODAY

"Dream big, it's the first step to success" - Anonymous

Date: /   /

THINGS TO BE GRATEFUL FOR TODAY

"A successful person is someone that understands temporary defeat as a learning process, never give up!"

Date: /   /

THINGS TO BE GRATEFUL FOR TODAY

"Motivation comes from working on our dreams and from taking action to achieve our goals"

Date: /   /

THINGS TO BE GRATEFUL FOR TODAY

> *"Dreams are the foundation to our imagination and success"*

Date: /   /

THINGS TO BE GRATEFUL FOR TODAY

> "Your mission in life should be to thrive and not merely survive"

Date: /   /

THINGS TO BE GRATEFUL FOR TODAY

> *"Doing what you believe in, and going after your dreams will only result in success."* - Anonymous

Date: /   /

THINGS TO BE GRATEFUL FOR TODAY

"The right time to start something new is now"

Date: /   /

THINGS TO BE GRATEFUL FOR TODAY

> *"Be brave, fight for what you believe in and make your dreams a reality."* - Anonymous

Date: /   /

THINGS TO BE GRATEFUL FOR TODAY

> *"Put more energy into your dreams than Into your fears and you will see positive results"*

Date: /   /

THINGS TO BE GRATEFUL FOR TODAY

"Let your dreams be bigger than your fears and your actions louder than your words." - Anonymous

Date: __ / __ / __

THINGS TO BE GRATEFUL FOR TODAY

> *"Always keep moving forward to keep your balance, if you stop dreaming you will fall"*

Date: /   /

THINGS TO BE GRATEFUL FOR TODAY

> *"Start every day with a goal in mind and make it happen with your actions"*

Date: /   /

THINGS TO BE GRATEFUL FOR TODAY

"Dream. Believe. Create. Succeed" - Anonymous

Date: /   /

THINGS TO BE GRATEFUL FOR TODAY

> *"You are never to old to set new goals and achieve them, keep on dreaming!"*

Date: /   /

THINGS TO BE GRATEFUL FOR TODAY

> *"If you have big dreams you will always have big reasons to wake up every day"*

Date: /   /

THINGS TO BE GRATEFUL FOR TODAY

> *"Difficulties are nothing more than opportunities in disguise, keep on trying and you will succeed"*

Date: /   /

THINGS TO BE GRATEFUL FOR TODAY

> *"To achieve our dreams we must first overcome our fear of failure"*

Date: /   /

THINGS TO BE GRATEFUL FOR TODAY

> *"Always have a powerful reason to wake up every new morning, set goals and follow your dreams"*

Date: /   /

THINGS TO BE GRATEFUL FOR TODAY

"Use failure as a motivation tool not as a sign of defeat"

Date: /   /

THINGS TO BE GRATEFUL FOR TODAY

> *"Never let your dreams die for fear of failure, defeat is just temporary; your dreams are your power"*

Date: /   /

THINGS TO BE GRATEFUL FOR TODAY

> *"A failure is a lesson, not a loss. It is a temporary and sometimes necessary detour, not a dead end"*

Date: /   /

THINGS TO BE GRATEFUL FOR TODAY

"Have faith in the future but above all in yourself"

Date: / /

THINGS TO BE GRATEFUL FOR TODAY

"Those who live in the past limit their future"
- Anonymous

Date: /   /

THINGS TO BE GRATEFUL FOR TODAY

> "Your future is created by what you do today not tomorrow" - Anonymous

Date: /   /

THINGS TO BE GRATEFUL FOR TODAY

"Never let your doubt blind your goals, for your future lies in your ability, not your failure" — *Anonymous*

Date: /   /

THINGS TO BE GRATEFUL FOR TODAY

"Don't go into something to test the waters, go into things to make waves" — Anonymous

Date: /   /

THINGS TO BE GRATEFUL FOR TODAY

> *"Laughter is the shock absorber that softens and minimizes the bumps of life"* — Anonymous

Date: /   /

THINGS TO BE GRATEFUL FOR TODAY

"Dream – Believe – Achieve"

Date: /   /

THINGS TO BE GRATEFUL FOR TODAY

"Make your own destiny. Don't wait for it to come to you, life is not a rehearsal" — Anonymous

Date: /   /

THINGS TO BE GRATEFUL FOR TODAY

"If you want to feel rich, just count all the things you have that money can't buy" — Anonymous

Date: /   /

THINGS TO BE GRATEFUL FOR TODAY

> *"Never give up on a dream just because of the time it will take to accomplish it. The time will pass anyway."* – Anonymous

Date: /   /

THINGS TO BE GRATEFUL FOR TODAY

> *"I am never a failure until I begin blaming others"*
> *- Anonymous*

Date: ___ / ___ / ___

THINGS TO BE GRATEFUL FOR TODAY

"Your only limitation is your imagination" — *Anonymous*

Date: /   /

THINGS TO BE GRATEFUL FOR TODAY

> *"Some pursue success and happiness – others create it"* — Anonymous

Date: /   /

THINGS TO BE GRATEFUL FOR TODAY

> *"Anything worth doing is worth doing well"*
> *— Anonymous*

Date: /   /

THINGS TO BE GRATEFUL FOR TODAY

> *"It's better to have an impossible dream than no dream at all."* – Anonymous

Date: /   /

THINGS TO BE GRATEFUL FOR TODAY

"Never let defeat have the last word" — *Anonymous*

Date: /   /

THINGS TO BE GRATEFUL FOR TODAY

"The winner always has a plan; The loser always has an excuse" — Anonymous

Date: /   /

THINGS TO BE GRATEFUL FOR TODAY

> *"There is no elevator to success.
> You have to take the stairs"* — Anonymous

Date: /   /

THINGS TO BE GRATEFUL FOR TODAY

"Don't let yesterday's disappointments, overshadow tomorrow's achievements" — *Anonymous*

Date: /   /

THINGS TO BE GRATEFUL FOR TODAY

> *"We are limited, not by our abilities, but by our vision"*
> — *Anonymous*

Date: /   /

THINGS TO BE GRATEFUL FOR TODAY

> *"Dreams don't come true. Dreams are true"*
> — Anonymous

Date: /   /

THINGS TO BE GRATEFUL FOR TODAY

> "Happiness is not something you get, but something you do" — Anonymous

Date: /   /

THINGS TO BE GRATEFUL FOR TODAY

> *"A journey of a thousand miles must begin with a single step."* – Lao Tzu

Date: /   /

THINGS TO BE GRATEFUL FOR TODAY

"Try and fail, but don't fail to try" — Anonymous

Date: /   /

THINGS TO BE GRATEFUL FOR TODAY

"You risk more when you don't take any risks"

Date: /   /

THINGS TO BE GRATEFUL FOR TODAY

> *"A diamond is a chunk of coal that made good under pressure"* — Anonymous

Date: /   /

THINGS TO BE GRATEFUL FOR TODAY

> *"No dreamer is ever too small; no dream is ever too big."* – Anonymous

Date: /   /

THINGS TO BE GRATEFUL FOR TODAY

"All our tomorrows depend on today" — *Anonymous*

Date: /   /

THINGS TO BE GRATEFUL FOR TODAY

> *"Remember yesterday, dream of tomorrow, but live for today"* — Anonymous

Date: /   /

THINGS TO BE GRATEFUL FOR TODAY

"Dream is not what you see in sleep, dream is the thing which does not let you sleep" — Anonymous

Date: /   /

THINGS TO BE GRATEFUL FOR TODAY

> *"Don't be pushed by your problems.
> Be led by your dreams"* — Anonymous

Date: /   /

THINGS TO BE GRATEFUL FOR TODAY

> *"Dreams give purpose to your life and meaning to your existence"*

Date: /   /

THINGS TO BE GRATEFUL FOR TODAY

> *"Once you have a dream put all your heart and soul to achieve it"*

Date: /   /

THINGS TO BE GRATEFUL FOR TODAY

"Follow your heart and your dreams will come true"
– Anonymous

Date: /   /

THINGS TO BE GRATEFUL FOR TODAY

> *"You create your life by following your dreams with decisive actions"*

Date: /   /

THINGS TO BE GRATEFUL FOR TODAY

> *"Without dreams you lose interest in life, you have no energy to move forward"*

Date: /   /

THINGS TO BE GRATEFUL FOR TODAY

"Difficult roads often lead to beautiful destinations"

Date: /   /

THINGS TO BE GRATEFUL FOR TODAY

> *"The road to success is always full of surprises and temporary failures, real success comes to those who persist"*

Date: /   /

THINGS TO BE GRATEFUL FOR TODAY

"Believe in yourself and you will be unstoppable"

Date: /   /

THINGS TO BE GRATEFUL FOR TODAY

"Today is another chance to get better"

Date: /   /

THINGS TO BE GRATEFUL FOR TODAY

> *"To live a creative life, we must lose our fear of being wrong"* - Anonymous

Date: /   /

THINGS TO BE GRATEFUL FOR TODAY

> *"Make each day count, you will never have this day again"*

Date: /   /

THINGS TO BE GRATEFUL FOR TODAY

> *"If you do what you always did,
> you will get what you always got"* - Anonymous

Date: /   /

THINGS TO BE GRATEFUL FOR TODAY

"It's not what you look at that matters, it's what you see" - Anonymous

Date: /   /

THINGS TO BE GRATEFUL FOR TODAY

"You are capable of amazing things"

Date: /   /

THINGS TO BE GRATEFUL FOR TODAY

"Believe in yourself and you will be unstoppable"

Date: /   /

THINGS TO BE GRATEFUL FOR TODAY

> *"Successful people make a habit of doing what unsuccessful people don't want to do"*
> *— Anonymous*

Date: /   /

THINGS TO BE GRATEFUL FOR TODAY

> *"To be the best you must be able to handle the worst"* - Anonymous

Date: /   /

THINGS TO BE GRATEFUL FOR TODAY

"Nothing worth having comes easy" - Anonymous

Date: /   /

THINGS TO BE GRATEFUL FOR TODAY

"Follow your dreams, they know the way"

Date: /   /

THINGS TO BE GRATEFUL FOR TODAY

"Don't Ever Give Up!"

Date: /   /

_____
_____
_____
_____
_____
_____
_____
_____
_____
_____
_____
_____
_____
_____
_____
_____
_____
_____
_____
_____

THINGS TO BE GRATEFUL FOR TODAY

We hope you enjoyed your journal – notebook, please let us know if you liked it by writing a review, it means a lot to us.
Thank you!

DESIGNED BY CREATIVE GIFTS STUDIO FOR:

CREATIVE JOURNALS FACTORY

FIND OTHER BEAUTIFUL JOURNALS, DIARIES AND NOTEBOOKS AT:

www.CreativeJournalsFactory.com

JOURNALS - DIARIES - NOTEBOOKS - COLORING BOOKS

Made in the USA
Monee, IL
07 August 2020